ON TRIAL

BUS AND COACH DEMONSTRATORS

Richard Walter

AMBERLEY

Front cover: Lothian Buses trialled MCV Volvo BZL demonstrator BV23 NNT with fleet number 997 in 2023 on a variety of city routes, such as service 9 as pictured, to see how it would cope with different road conditions.

Back cover: PO68 CAX is a UNVI Urbis PO50/17F partial open-top electric bus in London which was new to the RATP Original Extrapolitan sightseeing fleet (now rebranded as Tootbus) in October 2018.

First published 2024

Amberley Publishing
The Hill, Stroud
Gloucestershire, GL5 4EP

www.amberley-books.com

ISBN 978 1 3981 0708 3 (print)
ISBN 978 1 3981 0709 0 (ebook)

British Library Cataloguing in Publication Data.
A catalogue record for this book is available from the British Library.

Typesetting by SJmagic DESIGN SERVICES, India.
Printed in the UK.

Contents

Introduction

The post-Covid-19 pandemic years have proved to be a very volatile time for bus and coach operators with some companies and indeed manufacturers leaving the market and new ones entering it. Financial affairs, zero-emission desires and initiatives and most importantly passenger usage have been important factors in submitting future orders.

The Alexander Dennis 'Enviro' range was designed to meet carbon-emission requirements, and this Enviro100H demonstrator carries all of the important messages. Note, however, the unusual rear-door layout which was never incorporated in future models for health and safety reasons when the door opened outwards. (Tommy McReynolds)

The industry has always looked on trialling new types of vehicles as a good way of testing what is on the market, and now even more than ever there is a desire to buy wisely with electric and hydrogen products very much in favour as long as necessary infrastructures are in place. In days gone by, there weren't quite the same pressures but operators still liked to borrow different types of buses and coaches to put them through their paces.

This book looks mainly at more recently delivered demonstrators (with the principal focus on Scottish operators as that is where I am based), illustrating not only factory-new demonstrators but also buses borrowed from other UK operators. Some of these loans would lead to orders being made, others were promptly returned with no further interest. It also documents examples of new vehicles that were launched at UK events such as Euro Bus Expo and various coach shows and bus-operator events. By way of contrast, there is also a chapter which includes examples of some of the many demonstrators from the past.

During their time with various operators, demonstrators are often trialled on different routes and in varying road and traffic conditions. There is a specific chapter showing how buses are put through their paces – especially electric, hydrogen and autonomous buses as companies strive to move towards zero emissions.

The future is uncertain in the current volatile climate, but as new manufacturers come along with a variety of brand-new products on offer, and demand changes in terms of vehicle size and capabilities, the bus and coach scene is constantly evolving. I am sure that as soon as this book hits the shelves, there will already have been many developments and orders for varying types of body and chassis. In the meantime, I hope that you will enjoy this selection of images of colourful and sometimes unique vehicles.

I would like to thank the following fellow bus photographers for allowing me to use some of their excellent pictures: Gavin Booth, Andrew Chalmers, Stuart Dobie, Scott Hutchison, Donald MacRae, Tommy McReynolds, Ray Parnaby, Richard Sharman, Donald Stirling, Alistair Train and Jonathan Welch. Their work is duly acknowledged within the book.

And, finally, if you would like to see some other demonstrators and unique buses and coaches past and present, I recommend another Amberley Publishing title, *Demonstration, Trial & Experimental Buses* by Malcolm Batten.

Richard Walter
June 2024

1. On Trial – Putting Demonstrators Through Their Paces

Lochs Motor Transport borrowed ADL Enviro400 demonstrator SK71 CKX in late summer 2023. It was the first double-deck bus ever to be used in public service in the Western Isles. (Steven Macaskill)

The double-deck was used on school and local services and coped well with the narrow bends and roads of the Isle of Lewis. (Steven Macaskill)

Despite what it says on the screen, the bus was not reversing along the Braighe on its journey towards Point from Stornoway. The Braighe is a narrow stretch of land linking Point (Eye Peninsula) and the villages of Branahuie and Melbost. To the north of the Braighe road there is a sandy beach and to the south a pebble beach. (Steven Macaskill)

ADL Enviro400 SK71 CKX passes by the town hall in the centre of Stornoway towards the local bus station. It provoked much reaction from the public, who were unaccustomed to seeing a double-deck bus appearing across the island. (Donald Macarthur)

Lothian Buses trialled MCV Volvo BZL demonstrator BV23 NNT with fleet number 997 in 2023 on a variety of city routes to see how it would cope with different road conditions. It initially worked hilly route 23 from Trinity to Greenbank.

Lothian 997 was also used on service 8 from Muirhouse to the Royal Infirmary of Edinburgh – a busy cross-city service. Internally, the vehicle has full Lothian specification including seat and floor coverings, etc.

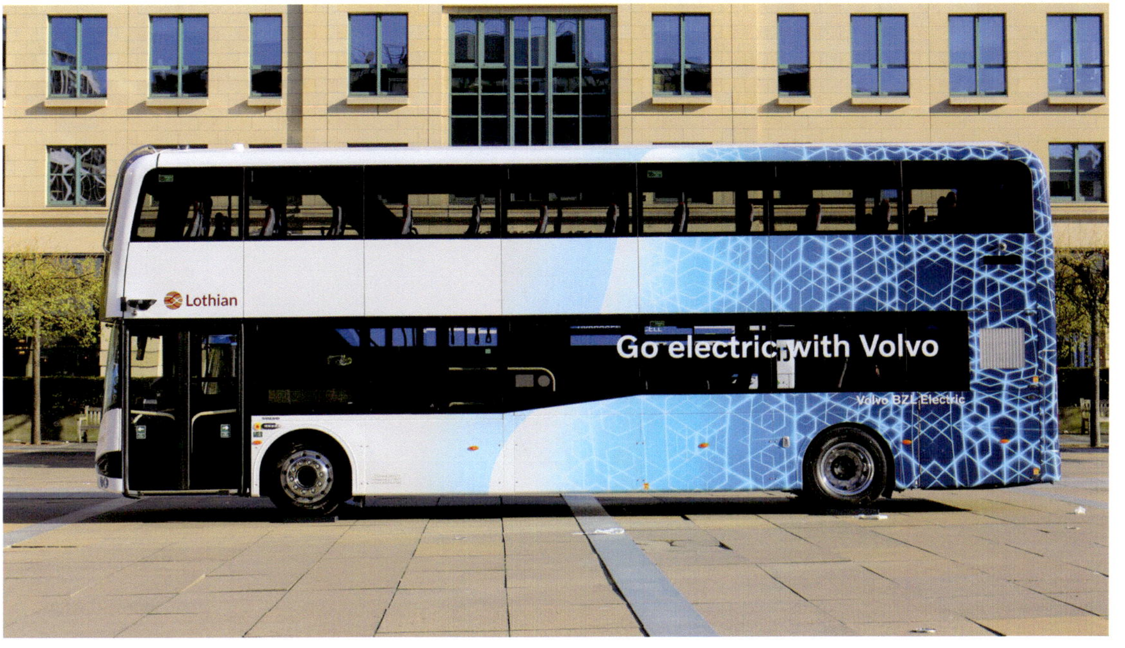

Lothian 997 received distinctive vinyls to its white livery in time for its appearance at the 2023 ALBUM Conference in Edinburgh. Held at the Sheraton Grand Hotel & Spa, the two-day conference featured contributions from various experts within and outside of the industry. A number of zero-emission buses, such as 997, were displayed at the event.

Lothian 997 also performed some duties on service 22 from The Gyle to Waterloo Place at the west end of Edinburgh.

Lothian 997 at Bristo Square, Edinburgh, heading towards Muirhouse on service 9. A full charge in the morning kept it on the road throughout the day.

Lothian 997 was photographed leaving King's Buildings in Edinburgh on route 9. This is the terminus for the University of Edinburgh. As a result of the trials of the bus, Lothian placed an order for fifty MCV Volvo BZLs to be delivered in 2024.

MCV Volvo BZL BV23 NNT was also one of three trial electric buses for McGill's Buses Xplore Dundee during 2023 to compare the performance of each on cross-city services such as the 5 and 5/A.

First South Yorkshire evaluated MCV Volvo BZL BV23 NNT as their 39601, seen here performing a special shuttle-bus service to take ticket holders to see the *Flying Scotsman* locomotive in November 2023.

The single-deck MCV Volvo BZL was also trialled by Lothian as their number 999 (BV72 KPF) mainly on service 1, which runs between Seafield and Clermiston. This route has been used for many demonstrator buses over the years.

999 heads into Edinburgh centre from the terminus of service 1 at Seafield.

As with 997 mentioned earlier, 999 was given a makeover during its stay for its appearance at the 2023 ALBUM Conference in Edinburgh.

During its time with Lothian, 999 proved to be a good performer in all weather conditions.

Lothian Buses also trialled Wrightbus Electroliner (LY71 GJE) which was used on a number of city routes, including the 24. It was numbered 998 on its third trial.

Lothian Buses had three loans of Wrightbus StreetDeck Electroliner (LY71 GJE) to evaluate at different times of the year. On its first two visits it carried the fleet number 997.

Wrightbus StreetDeck Electroliner (LY71 GJE) electric angel for Go North East, numbered 9048. (Ray Parnaby)

McGill's Buses Xplore Dundee also trialled the bus as its second electric demonstrator in 2023.

Seen in Dunbar, East Lothian, on its eleven-day Road to Renewables tour was a newly built and at that time unregistered pure-electric BYD ADL Enviro400EV customer demonstrator in a distinctive purple wrap for the COP26 UN Climate Change Conference in Glasgow.

The bus also stopped off in Edinburgh at the Scottish Parliament at Holyrood.

The unique Go-Ahead London General TA1 (LX18 DGF). This vehicle is a tri-axle Chinese bus with built-in air-conditioned BCI bodywork.

To date this has been the only tri-axle bus Transport for Scotland has operated in public service.

Mainly to be found on service 12 (Whitehall to Dulwich Library), the bus spent a fair bit of time off the road during its stay with London General.

TA1 was delivered to the Go-Ahead Camberwell garage from Ensign Bus' stewardship on 17 July 2018.

Among the many operators it visited in 2017, Wrightbus Streetlite Micro Hybrid3 SK17 HHL spent some time with Lothian Buses. It is seen here approaching Holyrood Park on short service 6 from City Centre to Scottish Government at Holyrood. Its distinctive 'lined' livery was hard to miss.

The bus crossing Princes Street, again on service 6.

On longer route 1 on Lothian Road outside the Usher Hall en route to Clermiston.

The bus was also trialled on service 24 between the Royal Infirmary of Edinburgh and Granton.

Lothian evaluated Caetano City GoldMAN EcoCity 200 gas bus WX61 FXO in 2012 and numbered it 200 during its stay.

200 ran on busy route 49 between the Jewel and Rosewell in Midlothian.

The bus was powered by CNG (compressed natural gas). MAN worked in conjunction with the Gas Bus Alliance, an organisation which brought together producers of bio methane to clean it up and feed it into the natural gas network.

WX61 FXO also spent time with McGill's Buses. The EcoCity was part of the extensive MAN Lion's City range which was to be sold as a complete MAN product, although actually had an Alusuisse body built by Caetano on a conventional MAN chassis. (Tommy McReynolds)

As illustrated throughout this book, Borders Buses (West Coast Motors) trialled a number of demonstrators between 2017 and 2019 including Optare MetroCity V1152MMC xFE YJ17 FXE. (Alistair Train)

Another view of the vehicle in its distinctive orange and white livery.

Borders Buses trialled Irizar i4 Hybrid coach demonstrator YN67 VCZ from its Galashiels depot on service X95 (Edinburgh to Carlisle), seen approaching Shawfair and passing the Sheriffhall Park and Ride site.

An evening shot of the coach in Princes Street, Edinburgh. The vehicle is DAF-powered and was the first hybrid coach in the UK. It was allocated fleet number 41705 for its visit.

PO68 CAX is a UNVI Urbis PO50/17F partial open-top electric bus in London which was new to the RATP Original Extrapolitan sightseeing fleet (now rebranded as Tootbus) in October 2018.

Initially, the bus was one of an order for ten battery-powered 12-m seventy-five-seat single-door UNVI Urbis double-decks. At the time of writing this book, no other such vehicles have entered service, although electric open-toppers are due in 2024 for West Coast Motors in Glasgow and McGill's Bright Bus in Edinburgh.

The bus was delivered in standard blue, red and white livery but now carries a green version of The Original Tour's Union Jack-inspired livery. It has a range of up to 150 km (93 miles) after a full charge (approximately 4 hours 30 minutes) using a charging point at Wandsworth garage where the fleet is based.

The electric open-topper was able to complete six circuits of The Original Tour's flagship Yellow Tour between charges, making 125 stops in 11 hours 30 minutes.

Switch Mobility MetroCity EV YJ19 HUV was loaned to Glasgow Citybus (West Coast Motors) during COP26 in October 2021. It operated on service 398 connecting Glasgow's Queen Street and Central train stations and Buchanan Street bus station.

Another view of Switch Mobility MetroCity EV YJ19 HUV. Note the clever variation to the usual Co-op signage to tie in with the COP26 events.

Also on loan to Glasgow Citybus for service 398 during COP26 was Switch Mobility MetroDecker EV MD1050 YJ19 HVC.

The bus was new as Metroline's OME2652 and also demonstrated with Go North East.

Switch Mobility MetroDecker EV MD1050 YJ19 HVC also ran in service in Edinburgh on Lothian Buses service 23.

The bus leaves the suburban area of Trinity heading into Edinburgh city centre.

At the end of 2023, Pelican Yutong had two U11DD electric demonstrators in service with various operators including First South Yorkshire, this one carrying the rather appropriate registration UU11 DDD. (Jonathan Welch)

Pelican Yutong U11DD (UU11 DDD) was the third electric demonstrator with McGill's Buses Xplore Dundee at the end of 2023, being demonstrated on a number of routes.

The U11DD is the first ever double-deck bus built in China to be imported and is a fully integral vehicle designed with low total cost of ownership in mind. YD73 FTP was trialled by Go North East on its Angel 21 service.

UU11 DDD is one of two demonstrators that were made available for operators to inspect at the end of 2023. YD73 FTP was one of the two demonstrators that were made available for operators to inspect at the end of 2023/early 2024.

Mercedes-Benz Citaro K BN17 JVC in September 2017 approaching Dalkeith from Woodburn on Lothian Buses service 39 prior to its own East Coast Buses division taking over local services.

Lothian also used Mercedes-Benz Citaro K BN17 JVC on service 69 from King's Road to Willowbrae.

Borders Buses ADL Enviro400 MMC 11801 (YX67 UXB) leaving Galashiels Transport Interchange in original demonstration livery. The operator acquired the vehicle, and it now appears in fleet livery.

11801 passing through Penicuik on its long journey to Edinburgh from Galashiels.

Prentice of Haddington trialled ADL Enviro200 MMC YX18 KWV on service 108, seen passing through Musselburgh.

Prentice of Haddington trialled a number of ADL Enviro200 MMCs and subsequently ordered quite a few for the fleet.

Yutong E12 YTM280 zero-emission battery electric bus YK66 CBC was briefly demonstrated by Lothian in June 2018 on its service 1 between Clermiston and Easter Road.

The E12 is Yutong's 12.17-m full-electric zero-emission bus which has been operating in Europe for over five years and in the UK since 2017.

The vehicles are capable of a daily operational range of over 370 km on a single charge, subject to their specific operational conditions.

Yutong E12 YK66 CBC was also trialled by McGill's Buses during its spell in Scotland. (Tommy McReynolds)

During summer 2023, Ratho Coaches trialled Zeelo Yutong TCe12 electric demonstrator coach YD72 FEM.

Among other duties, the Yutong TCe12 performed contract work in Glasgow and Edinburgh for Amazon employees.

The success of the demonstrator led to Ratho Coaches purchasing similar Yutong TCe12 SG73 TZA later in the year. It is seen here at South Queensferry when new.

Ratho Coaches Yutong TCe12 SG73 TZA posing in front of the Forth Road Bridge.

In 2014, Lothian Buses trialled demonstrator Wright Gemini 3-bodied Volvo B5TL BF63 HDC, which was given fleet number 286. It was used mainly on service 27 and was photographed here approaching the Hunter's Tryst terminus on its journey from Silverknowes.

Copyright issues over the style of glazed staircases on the Wright-bodied New Routemasters for London meant that this demonstrator featured a rather unattractive layout. This was vastly improved for future Lothian orders following trial of 286.

286 passing one of Lothian's large fleet of Wrightbus Geminis crossing from Hanover Street onto The Mound in Edinburgh.

In addition to trialling the bus on service 27, Lothian Buses allocated the vehicle to other routes such as rush service X12 from Waterloo Place to Ingliston.

2. On Show – Displaying New Models to Operators and the Media

Dawsongroup Bus and Coach-liveried ADL Enviro400 on display at Coach & Bus UK in 2019. The company is a leading supplier for the UK road-passenger transport sector.

Go North East 5498 (NK69 FBN), an ADL Enviro200 MMC, was shown at Coach & Bus UK in 2019 prior to entering service with the operator.

Volvo B11RLE Plaxton Panorama on show when new at Coach & Bus UK in 2019.

The vehicle subsequently moved to Park's of Hamilton as its LSK 807, retaining its demonstrator livery until the end of 2023 when it was painted into Citylink colours. (Andrew Chalmers)

Pelican Yutongs with Traw Cymru (E12) and Newport Transport (E10) were displayed at Euro Bus Expo in 2022, showing different styles of roofline. Both are fitted with camera mirror systems.

This Mellor Sigma 8 demonstrator was displayed at Euro Bus Expo in 2022. The 8.5-m model offers a fifty-four-passenger capacity.

Also shown was a Mellor Sigma 10 version, which was available for demonstration outside the exhibition halls.

Looking immaculate in the famous Yelloway livery, seen here is the combination of a Beulas Cygnus body on a VDL SB4000 chassis.

The BYD ADL Enviro400EV zero-emission bus is now common in the UK. LF69 UXJ has been demonstrated across the UK and was photographed at the Coach & Bus UK event at the Birmingham NEC in 2019.

LF69 UXJ was outside the exhibition arena to allow closer inspection and short trips.

Pelican Bus & Coach showed off this Yutong fully-electric E10 demonstrator in London livery at the Coach & Bus UK event at the Birmingham NEC in 2019.

The bus was painted in what had become the traditional livery of red with green leaves to indicate zero-emission vehicles.

Go Ahead London are expected to roll out twenty of these new emission-free electric Irizar ie tram buses from spring 2024 on route 358 between Crystal Palace and Orpington.

Topped up via a 500-kW charger at each terminus point, the ie trams reflect Irizar's push to expand its UK presence.

The vehicles are 12.16 m long, which is indeed long for a London single-deck bus, and are fitted with a camera mirror system. The frontal design was modified to move the windscreen wipers to above the windscreen to meet TfL pedestrian safety standards.

Another Irizar ie tram being inspected by officials in central London in May 2023.

In summer 2017, York became the first UK city outside of London to trial fully-electric Optare MetroDecker EV YJ17 FXX. The bus is seen on display at the University of York prior to its trials with First York. (See also page 92 for a photo of it with London Central.)

First York trialled the bus on several different routes before ordering twenty-one similar battery-electric MetroDecker EVs, which were launched on 30 July 2020.

Harris Group Demonstrator Higer STEED (Sustainable Transport Electric Energy Delivered) with Transport for Ireland 211-D-15865 appeared at Euro Bus Expo 2022. These buses have been built specifically with narrow town roads and city centres in mind.

Airsym Yutong TCe12 EV72 SYM at Euro Bus Expo 2022. This is the vehicle that went on national trial. (See photos on pages 37 and 38.)

Alexander Dennis revealed its new hydrogen-powered Enviro400FCEV at the Euro Bus Expo in 2022. This example was destined for operation in Liverpool.

A much-travelled demonstrator is BYD ADL Enviro400EV LC71 EFD, in colourful zero-emissions branding.

Switch Mobility revealed an all-white version of its new e1 at the Euro Bus Expo in 2022. The 12-m low-floor bus with twenty-eight seats is the manufacturer's first fully-electric bus designed specifically for the European market.

A Cummins-engined AOS Grand Toro 37 for Newport Transport from EVM UK.

This BYD/ADL Enviro200EV 10.8 demonstrator was to become LJ68 CYO and was trialled by a number of operators across the UK, including Prentice of Haddington (see pages 92, 88).

A Switch Mobility MetroCity in its shortest length and with the latest TfL pedestrian impact safety features, seen again at the Euro Bus Expo 2022 event.

Another Alexander Dennis hydrogen-powered Enviro400FCEV demonstrator on display at the ALBUM 2023 Conference in Edinburgh.

Scania has developed the Fencer F1 which now sports a brand-new chassis and Euro VI Step E engine. This demonstrator appeared at the 2022 Euro Bus Expo in Birmingham.

Prior to undertaking a number of demonstrator duties across the UK, MCV Volvo BZL BV72 KPG appeared at the 2022 Euro Bus Expo in Birmingham.

First York Optare Versa 49912 (YJ15 AYO) at Birmingham NEC is an example of a repowered bus. It is one of twelve First York vehicles converted from existing 'Generation One' electrical systems to Equipmake's ZED.

3. Borrowing from Other Operators

Grampian Regional Transport tried out a number of buses from other operators such as Derby Northern Counties Volvo Citybus 148 (C148 NRR). (Donald MacRae)

Another borrowed vehicle by Grampian was Greater Manchester Buses Northern Counties-bodied Leyland Olympian 3276 (D276 JVR). (Donald MacRae)

Newport Transport Scania 29 (C29 ETG), an East Lancs-bodied Scania N112DR with Grampian, in not too different fleet colours. (Donald MacRae)

South Yorkshire Alexander Dennis Dominator 2485 (D485 OWE) was another vehicle that spent some time with Grampian. (Donald MacRae)

Pictured in York Place in July 1993 on hire to ESOL is Tayside V247 (K247 HKV), a 1993 Northern Counties Volvo B10B. (Gavin Booth)

Inspected by Lothian Buses management, but not used in service, was London Hybrid HV3 (LJ09 KOH), photographed leaving Central Garage. (Donald Stirling)

A visitor to the 2014 Lothian Buses Open Doors event at the company's Central Garage was then brand-new Wrightbus New Routemaster for London LT299 (LTZ 1299). It did not get trialled in service.

Former London Buses Alexander Mercedes 811D F679 XMS in Musselburgh while on loan to SMT.

In London-style livery is Plaxton Verde-bodied Dennis Lance demonstrator J120 SPF on loan to Tayside. The design of body, new in 1991, boasted split-entrance steps, high-visibility handrails and the now common interior 'Bus Stopping' signs. (Donald MacRae)

Tayside East Lancs Dennis DD159 Dominator 280 (JSL 280X) during its spell on loan to Grampian. (Donald MacRae)

4. Demonstrators Old and New

ADL Enviro400H SN59 AWW is a hybrid-powered example in demonstrator livery. (Tommy McReynolds)

Wrightbus Eclipse Gemini Volvo B7TL in demonstrator livery. (Tommy McReynolds)

Demonstrator Optare Delta DA G684 KNW on loan to Lothian Region Transport (LRT) at the Findlay Gardens terminus of service 13.

Pictured in St Andrew Square, Edinburgh, is Wright Dart demonstrator LDZ 6040 with Lothian Region Transport (LRT).

Wright MAN Meridian W08 SWK was the only dual-door example of the low number of Meridian bodies built after 2007. It was borrowed by Arriva Scotland West for use on its Glasgow Flyer Airport service. It was later converted to a more conventional single-door bus. (Tommy McReynolds)

In 2007, ADL launched its new Enviro300 demonstrator SN57 DXC, pictured in service with Arriva. (Tommy McReynolds)

Henderson Travel/SPT Hybrid ADL Enviro200 SN11 BLV. (Tommy McReynolds)

ADL Enviro400 SN60 CAA, which became 8960 in the McGill's Buses fleet. (Tommy McReynolds)

Transbus ADL Enviro300 SK52 USS was inspected by Lothian Buses in its green and blue demonstration livery but was not used in service.

In 2013, Mercedes-Benz Citaro demonstrator BX02 CMK worked briefly on Lothian Buses service 13 from Blackhall to Lochend.

During 2021, McGill's Buses borrowed and operated National Car Parks' BYD ADL Enviro200EVs, including EV2 (LF69 UXM) originally bought for Long Stay Car Park duties at Glasgow Airport. It is seen en route to Clydebank on service 757. (Tommy McReynolds)

ADL Enviro300 School Bus SN56 AXM, on display in the centre of Glasgow. (Tommy McReynolds)

Henderson Travel Optare Solo M780SE Green Bus 257 YJ57 XXC. (Tommy McReynolds)

The Optare East Lancashire Esteem was a low-floor single-deck body – and in the case of this demonstrator, on a Scania chassis. (Tommy McReynolds)

Wright Crusader Volvo B6RLE T290 ROF while on demonstration with Whitelaws Coaches. (Tommy McReynolds)

The Plaxton Pointer (originally known as the Reeve Burgess Pointer and later as the TransBus Pointer and Alexander Dennis Pointer (as in photo)) was manufactured during the 1990s by Reeve Burgess, Plaxton and latterly built by Alexander Dennis. (Plaxton with thanks to Gavin Booth)

Caetano Nimbus-bodied Dennis Dart V674 FPO in a very bright demonstrator livery with Lothian Region Transport (LRT) at the Findlay Gardens terminus of service 13.

Scania OmniCity demonstrator YR10 BBO when new ended up with Sanders Coaches where it suffered a serious engine fire in March 2017. (Tommy McReynolds)

London Transport Leyland B15 BCK 706R at its press launch in Coventry in 1977 when the Titan name was revealed. (Gavin Booth)

Volvo B7LA demonstrator FJ53 LZX with Spanish-built Hispano bodywork arrived at Lothian Buses during 2005 in London red and was subsequently disguised in the harlequin vinyls applied to the operator's own vehicles. Due to its length, it was restricted to routes it could operate on (19 and 26) and had to be garaged at Marine Depot.

The Optare Vecta was introduced in 1991 on a version of the MAN 11-180 chassis. (Optare with thanks to Gavin Booth)

Optare Tempo YK57 FHM in distinctive demonstrator livery. The Tempo was an integral low-floor, full-size, single-deck bus manufactured by Optare and launched in late 2004. (Tommy McReynolds)

Mercedes-Benz O405 Optare Prisma M925 TYG. The body was constructed from Alusuisse aluminium alloy. (Optare with thanks to Gavin Booth)

Optare Versa YJ57 EHU. This is a low-floor midibus that was manufactured by Optare at its Sherburn-in-Elmet factory. In total 883 were produced between 2007 and 2018. (Tommy McReynolds)

Nottingham City Transport BYD ADL Enviro400 DD18 GAS is the operator's hundredth gas type. (Tommy McReynolds)

Plaxton R739 TMO, seen here while with Trentbarton, was the first production Super Pointer Dart which was the 11.3-m version of the Dart SLF. (Plaxton with thanks to Gavin Booth)

During 2008, Lothian operated ex-demonstrator Scania CN94UA artic 50 (YN54 ALO) on Park & Ride service X48 alongside similarly branded Dennis Darts and Plaxton Tridents.

NHG 732P, a B15/Park Royal H44/27D new in 1975, on demonstration with Preston Borough in 1981. (Gavin Booth)

The rather attractive Hispano Habit Volvo B7L was new as a demonstrator and ended up with McGill's Buses as 228 (BX03 OVZ). (Tommy McReynolds)

ADL Enviro200 MMC demonstrator YX65 RLO spent a week on loan to Prentice of Haddington in September 2016, when it was photographed at Musselburgh Tesco.

Another ADL Enviro200 MMC (YY64 YKC) was also trialled by Prentice of Haddington. (Stuart Dobie)

Dennis Lance J110 SPB was a rear-engine single-deck chassis. It was painted in SMT (Eastern Scottish) colours and was first seen at the Coach & Bus Show in 1991. (Gavin Booth)

McGill's Buses ran demonstrator Wrightbus Streetlite ERZ 2028. (Tommy McReynolds)

ADL Enviro400 SN59 AWV on trial with McGill's Buses was numbered 901. (Tommy McReynolds)

Formerly a demonstrator, this ADL Enviro400 ended up as McGill's Buses J8960 (SN59 AWX). (Tommy McReynolds)

Wright StreetDeck Hybrid Electric 40715 (SK18 TKX) with Diamond Bus North West in Wrightbus Demonstrator Livery was pictured in Manchester. (Ray Parnaby)

Wright StreetDeck 40700 (SK17 HHC) with Diamond Bus North West in another Wrightbus Demonstrator Livery was photographed in Manchester, Piccadilly. (Ray Parnaby)

ADL-bodied Scania N113CRB G113 SKX was trialled by a number of operators and is seen here while on loan to Northern Scottish. (Donald MacRae)

Go-Ahead Wrightbus GB Kite Hydroliner 6057 (LV23 EDU) is used on Metrobus Fastway services in the Crawley, Redhill and Gatwick Airport area.

All-electric Carbon Battle Bus Yutong ZKH coach EL19 TRC in Glasgow during COP26 in 2021 as part of its 'Race to Zero' campaign.

Colchri Coaches Ltd took delivery of four Hybrid ADL Enviro200s in summer 2011, the first to operate in Scotland. SN11 BVD was one example. (Tommy McReynolds)

McGill's Buses had on loan Optare MetroCity YJ64 DWK, which was a regular on service 101. (Tommy McReynolds)

Optare Solo xFE OP14 ARE in Tavistock bus station on hire to Beacon Bus and heading north to Okehampton. (Alistair Train)

Eve's of Dunbar put ADL Enviro200 MMC YX69 NZD through its paces on local services in East Lothian. (Stuart Dobie)

Silver-liveried Wrightbus StreetDeck SN64 CTU demonstrator, new in January 2015, became 9119 with Go North East. It is pictured here in the centre of Newcastle.

Demonstrator Optare MetroDecker YJ16 DBO initially ran with Go-Ahead London Central but was loaned to First York during 2021 when it was given fleet number 35006.

First York also borrowed similar widely travelled Optare MetroDecker YJ65 EPU, which was numbered 35005 while in service in York.

Volvo B11R/MCV EvoTor BV19 LMJ was new to Ridley's Leamington Spa but later acted as a demonstrator for Volvo and is seen here while working with Park's of Hamilton. (Scott Hutchison)

During 2012, Lothian Buses had a visit from Hong Kong Alexander Dennis Enviro500. It is seen here following the route of Airlink service 100, albeit without fare-paying passengers.

Lothian Motorcoaches trialled Mercedes-Benz Tourismo BF68 ZGS in summer 2019. The coach is seen on a tour heading up Market Street to The Mound, Edinburgh.

Borders Buses trialled ADLEnviro400 City SN66 WLK, photographed leaving Edinburgh on its trek into the Borders. The bus ended up being bought by Courtney Buses and painted in Milton Park livery for use in Reading. (Stuart Dobie)

Borders Buses demonstrator Mercedes-Benz Citaro BT66 TZE on layover in Edinburgh bus station.

Reading Buses borrowed demonstrator Scania N250UD/AD Enviro400 MMC 778 (YN16 CFU), seen leaving Victoria, London. This bus was later to become Borders Buses yellow and blue tartan 'My Name's Doddie' campaign-vinyled 11622.

Following trial by Lothian Buses of MCV Volvo eVoRa 299 (BV19 LND), the company ordered fifty similar vehicles.

Prentice of Haddington evaluated BYD ADL Enviro200EV demonstrator LJ68 CYO in June 2021 on a number of services in East Lothian, including the 111 which operates from Haddington to the Royal Infirmary of Edinburgh. The bus is seen here heading to Stoneybank in Musselburgh.

In 2003, Lothian experimented with Optare Solo YF02 SKU on short city-centre service C60.

Borders Buses had on loan ADL Enviro200 303 (YX19 DWA) in July 2019.

ADLEnviro400 SN61 DFK spent time with Lothian Buses in 2013 on service 10 between Western Harbour and Torphin.

An example of the stylish Neoplan Tourliner. The state-of-the-art colour design, superior-quality materials and all-over concept sets high standards in terms of travel comfort. (Scott Hutchison)

Widely travelled Mercedes-Benz eCitaro demonstrator M21 BUS spent a short time with McGill's Buses and in this photo was being evaluated on service 38 from Glasgow to Johnstone. (Scott Hutchison)

Tower Transit Wright Pulsar 2 Hydrogen VDL SB200 WSH 62992 (LK60 HPF) was one of a number of hydrogen buses used on the now withdrawn RV1 service from Tower Gateway to Covent Garden in London.

Tower Transit also operated two Van Hool A330FC Hydrogen Fuel Cell buses of which BH 63102 (LJ67 HTG) was one.

In 2016, Metroline operated five Chinese-built BYD electric buses – the first all-electric vehicles in the capital. BYD1471 (LJ16 EZM) was pictured on route 98, which they were allocated to. All five buses were sold in 2021.

London Central trialled Electric Optare MetroDecker MD1 (YJ17 FXX), which was later demonstrated by First York (see page 49).

5. Autonomous and Buses of the Future

The rather bizarre Dutch-built Amfibious bus took part in trials by Stagecoach between existing slipways at Renfrew and Yoker in February 2010. (Tommy McReynolds)

Another view of this unusual vehicle. The plan had been to introduce a new service linking the north and south bank of the Clyde which would also operate on roads between Braehead and Renfrew, but it was not to be. (Tommy McReynolds)

Originally planned to commence in 2020 prior to the Covid-19 pandemic, one of the five Stagecoach East Scotland Alexander Dennis Enviro200AV autonomous buses was used for demonstration purposes at the NEC Birmingham Coach & Bus UK event in 2019.

The autonomous vehicle going through its paces for visitors to the NEC.

By the time that trials of the CAVForth project service formally started in Fife in April 2022, the buses had picked up a distinctive bright new livery.

The long-awaited CAVForth project autonomous route AB1 commenced in May 2023. Stagecoach East Scotland Alexander Dennis Enviro200AV 62003 (YX69 NUP) reaches the Edinburgh Park terminus.

The Mellor Orion E electric autonomous bus (SJ71 HRM) commenced on 23 January 2023 at Milton Park in Didcot. (Richard Sharman)

A rear view of the vehicle leaving for its circuit of Milton Park. (Richard Sharman)